Food Field Trips

Let's Explore Honey!

Jill Colella

Lerner Publications ◆ Minneapolis

Hello, Friends,

Everybody eats, even from birth. This is why learning about food is important. Making the right choices about what to eat begins with knowing more about food. Food literacy helps us be curious about food and adventurous about what we eat. In short, it helps us discover how delicious the world of food can be.

Many sweet and yummy foods come from nature. Honey is one sticky and tasty example. My favorite way to eat honey is on toast. What about you?

For more inspiration, ideas, and recipes, visit www.teachkidstocook.com.

About the Author

Happy cook, reformed picky eater, and longtime classroom teacher Jill Colella founded both *Ingredient* and *Butternut*, award-winning children's magazines that promote food literacy.

Lerner Publications Company
An imprint of Lerner Publishing Group, Inc.
241 First Avenue North
Minneapolis, MN 55401 USA

For reading levels and more information, look up this title at www.lernerbooks.com.

Main body text set in Mikado. Typeface provided by HVD.

Library of Congress Cataloging-in-Publication Data

Names: Colella, Jill, 1975- author.
Title: Let's explore honey / by Jill Colella.
Description: Minneapolis, MN : Lerner Publications, [2020] | Series: Food field trips | Audience: Age 4-8. | Audience: K to Grade 3. | Includes bibliographical references and index.
Identifiers: LCCN 2019011667 (print) | LCCN 2019012985 (ebook) | ISBN 9781541582972 (eb pdf) | ISBN 9781541563032 (lib. bdg. : alk. paper)
Subjects: LCSH: Honey—Juvenile literature.
Classification: LCC SF539 (ebook) | LCC SF539 .C65 2020 (print) | DDC 638/.16—dc23

LC record available at https://lccn.loc.gov/2019011667

Manufactured in the United States of America
1-46465-47542-8/8/2019

SCAN FOR BONUS CONTENT!

Table of Contents

All about Honey. 4

Let's Compare 7

Let's Explore. 8

Let's Visit a Honey Farm . . . 11

Let's Cook. 20

Let's Make 22

Let's Read. 24

Index 24

Picture Glossary

ALL ABOUT HONEY

Honey is a sweet food made by honeybees. We put honey in foods such as granola, bread, cereal, and cookies.

Honey can be a topping or dip. Some people put honey on biscuits, toast, pancakes, cheese, and even ice cream.

Honey makes a delicious, natural snack.

LET'S COMPARE

Some foods are sweet, such as honey. Others are salty, spicy, or sour. Our tongues help us taste the difference. Which of these foods are sweet?

LET'S EXPLORE

Queen bees lay tiny eggs in honeycombs.

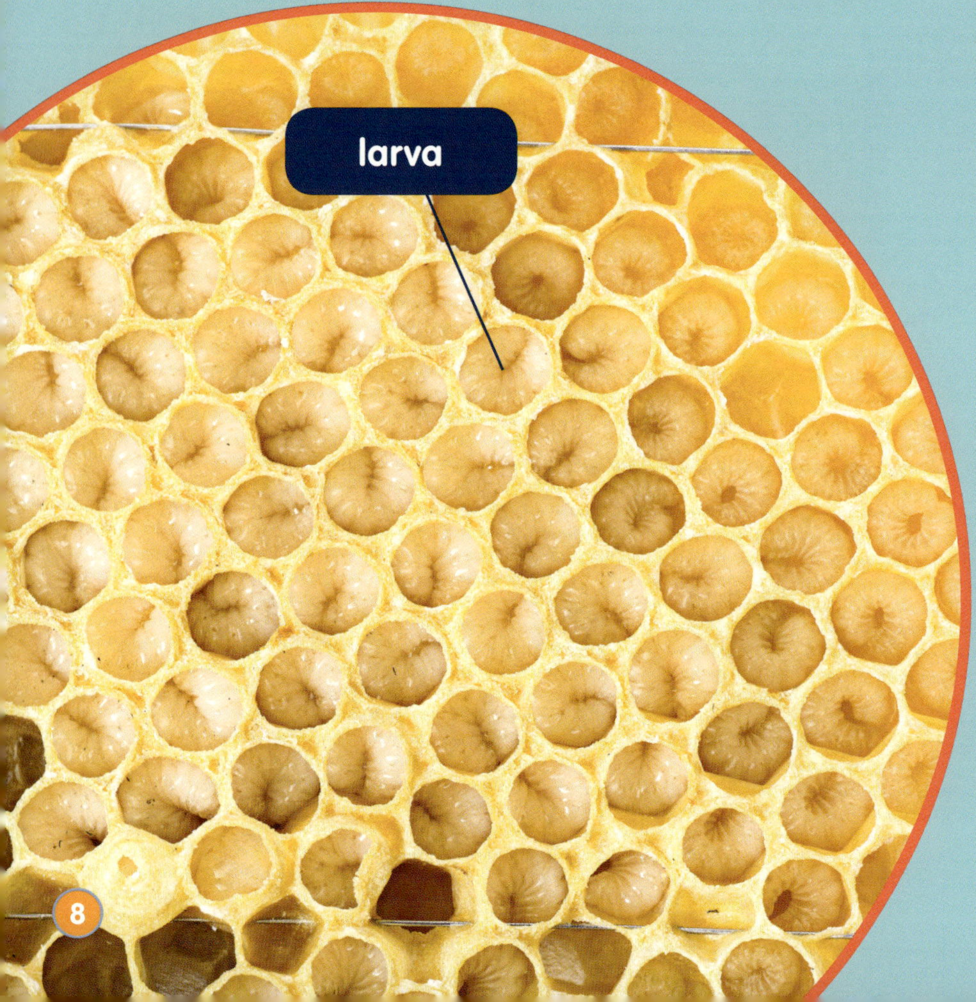

larva

When an egg hatches, a tiny larva crawls out. The larva eats pollen and nectar, and then it spins itself into a cocoon.

Then it becomes a pupa. Soon the pupa comes out of the cocoon. Some pupae become worker bees. These bees gather nectar from flowers and bring it back to the hive.

Inside the hive, the bees store nectar. The nectar gets stickier and sweeter, becoming honey. Bees keep the honey in their honeycomb. A beekeeper removes it for us to eat.

LET'S VISIT A HONEY FARM

Have you visited a farm? A farm that raises bees is an apiary.

This part of the apiary is a bee field.
Bees live in hives.

Why might a farmer take care of bees?

Bees build a hive inside a box. Hives are where the bees live. Never touch a hive!

Beekeepers help take care of the bees. They wear special clothes for safety.

A beekeeper opens the hive. Wooden frames are inside. She sprays the bees with smoke to keep them calm.

Why is it important for the bees to be calm?

The bees build waxy honeycombs in the frames. Lots of honey means that the bees are healthy.

To get the honey, the beekeeper removes the honeycomb. Then the frame goes inside a machine.

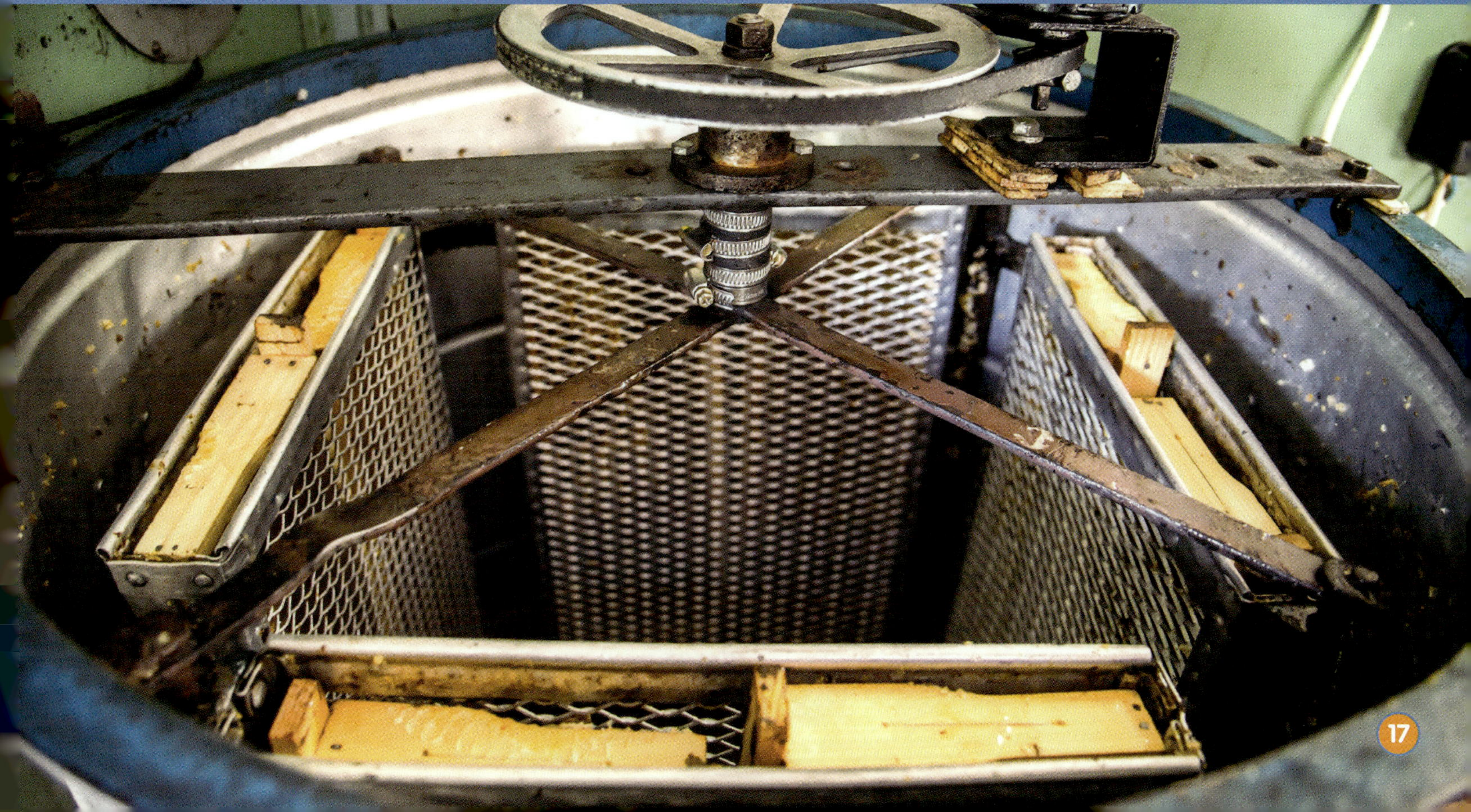

The machine spins the frame
to make the honey come out.
It goes into a big tank.

After the honey is strained and heated, it goes into bottles. Yum, it is ready to eat!

Why is the honey heated before it can be eaten?

LET'S COOK

Have this toast for breakfast or for a quick and easy snack. This recipe makes 1 serving.

HONEY BANANA TOAST

INGREDIENTS

- 1 slice of your favorite bread
- 2 teaspoons honey
- ½ of a banana, sliced into rounds

1. With an adult's help, put bread in a toaster or toaster oven and toast.
2. Spread honey over the toast.
3. Top with banana slices.
4. If you wish, add a sprinkle of granola or chocolate chips for more crunch or sweetness.

SEE THIS RECIPE IN ACTION!

LET'S MAKE

This fun craft lets you make your own beehive, complete with pollen and nectar!

BUILD A BEEHIVE

MATERIALS

- empty egg carton
- scissors
- white and yellow paint
- paintbrushes
- craft glue
- yellow tissue paper
- mini yellow pompoms

1. Collect an empty egg carton.
2. Cut the carton in half so there are six beehive cells.

3. Paint the outside white to look like a beehive box and the inside yellow to look like a honeycomb.

4. Glue in crumpled yellow tissue paper to be the nectar and yellow pompoms to be pollen.

5. If you wish, you can draw or make a bee to go inside the hive.

Let's Read

Hansen, Grace. *Help the Honey Bees*. Minneapolis: Abdo Kids Jumbo, 2019.

Honeybee Conservancy
https://thehoneybeeconservancy.org

Lukidis, Lydia. *The Broken Bees' Nest*. New York: Kane, 2018.

Macken, JoAnn Early. *Take a Closer Look at Bees*. Egremont, MA: Red Chair Press, 2016.

National Honey Board
https://www.honey.com

Owings, Lisa. *From Egg to Honeybee*. Minneapolis: Lerner Publications, 2017.

Index

apiary, 11–12

bee, 4, 16–24
beekeeper, 10, 14, 17

healthy, 16
honeycomb, 8, 10

larva, 8

nectar, 8–10

pupa, 9

Photo Acknowledgments

Image credits: Dawid G/Shutterstock.com, p. 1; Jupiterimages/PHOTOS.com/Getty Images, p. 3 (hive); ElementalImaging/E+/Getty Images, p. 3 (bee); nitrub/iStock/Getty Images, p. 3 (honey); Deb Nystrom/flickr (CC BY 2.0), p. 3 (flower); paulbein/iStock/Getty Images, p. 3 (pollen); da-kuk/E+/Getty Images, p. 4; DebbiSmirnoff/iStock/Getty Images, p. 5 (top); Volodymyr Plysiuk/Shutterstock.com, p. 5 (bottom left); photoviriya/Shutterstock.com, p. 5 (bottom right); IPGGutenbergUKLtd/iStock/Getty Images, p. 6; tashka2000/iStock/Getty Images, p. 7 (honey); ayala_studio/E+/Getty Images, p. 7 (pepper); rez-art/iStock/Getty Images, p. 7 (lemon juice); Miro Novak/Shutterstock.com, p. 7 (salt); Alter-ego/Shutterstock.com, p. 7 (jam); Daniel Wiedemann/Shutterstock.com, p. 7 (syrup); Kuttelvaserova Stuchelova/Shutterstock.com, p. 8 (larva); Inventori/iStock/Getty Images, p. 8 (eggs); Waugsberg/Wikimedia Commons (CC BY-SA 3.0), p. 9 (top); Paolo Negri/Photographer's Choice RF/Getty Images, p. 9 (bottom left); IdealPhoto30/iStock/Getty Images, p. 9 (bottom right); sergey kolesnikov/Shutterstock.com, p. 10; Warren-Pender/iStock/Getty Images, p. 11; Jacky Parker Photography/Moment/Getty Images, p. 12; Sushaaa/iStock/Getty Images, p. 13; Stefano Oppo/Cultura/Getty Images, p. 14; tomprout/E+/Getty Images, p. 15; guvendemir/iStock/Getty Images, p. 16; mladenbalinovac/iStock/Getty Images, p. 17 (top); yanik88/iStock/Getty Images, pp. 17 (bottom), 18; ClarkandCompany/iStock/Getty Images, p. 19 (top); takenobu/iStock/Getty Images, p. 19; Lia Buffa/iStock/Getty Images, p. 20; Laura Westlund/Independent Picture Service, pp. 21, 23 (illustrations); Jordyn Taylor/Todd Strand/Independent Picture Service, p. 22.

Front cover: Diyana Dimitrova/Shutterstock.com (honeycomb); Tatevosian Yana/Shutterstock.com (child); Olgysha/Shutterstock.com, (hives); New Africa/Shutterstock.com (pancakes). Back cover: weter78/Shutterstock.com.